CHOOSE YOUR WORDS
CHANGE YOUR WORLD

THE ANSWER YOU'VE BEEN LOOKING FOR IS RIGHT UNDER YOUR NOSE

DAVID LEE MARTIN

CONTENTS

THE BOOK OF EPHESIANS

The Book Of Colossians

The Book of Philippians

INTRODUCTION

"A wholesome tongue is a tree of life"

— PROVERBS 15:4A

You are living today in the fruits of the words you spoke yesterday. The words that proceed from your heart pave the way for the steps you take into your tomorrow.

This reality is real and incredibly practical. It places you in the driving seat of your destiny.

Your tongue can release life.

Or death.

You decide.

Every time you open your mouth is a decision to direct your ship in one direction or another. Failure to take hold of your own words leaves you at the mercy of life's crashing waves. It's like taking your hand off the rudder and just letting the swirling waters drive you whichever way they will.

I believe it's time for you to take control. Your hand on the rudder, and God's hand on yours, with divine destiny firmly in sight.

This is how God designed it to be.

Choose your words carefully and send them before you in the direction you want your life to follow.

Right now, wherever you are, and whatever challenges you are facing, changing your words will change your world.

This is not mere philosophy. None of my books have been written as time fillers. They are poured on the page because I'm living in the messy middle - doing my best to get Bible truth into my here and now.

That's how this fresh study and practical application came into being.

At the time of writing, I was being starkly reminded in a very real way just how powerful our words are.

We all face circumstances that want to squeeze a wrong confession out of us. Words of defeat. Words of hopelessness. My own household was going through one of those seasons, and boy oh boy, did we face the temptation to speak the very things we did NOT want to see happen!

My emotions and my mind were almost begging for me to let rip with negativity (and I wish I could say I perfectly resisted!). It seemed that so much of what I had worked and prayed for was crumbling before me, and I knew a fresh approach had to be seized to turn things around.

I've learned over the past thirty years or so that there is only one rock on which you can stand when all your world is shaking - the Word of God.

How easy it is for us to slip from this reality in the busyness of life.

In fact, I am now thanking God sincerely for allowing the challenges that assaulted my comforts, because they threw me back to a place of renewed trust in the never-changing, ever-faithful Word of life, rather than my own flaky understanding!

And not just a few promise-box scriptures either. I've been swept into a whole new appreciation of how powerful and life-changing personalisation of the Scriptures can be.

Entire letters from the New Testament have burst into fresh life for me, and applying them through **consistent confession has opened up an entirely reformed**

vocabulary that I sense getting stronger every day to combat any fiery dart the enemy of my soul might throw at me.

Praying the Word is a sword that should be wielded by the hands of every Christian disciple. The principle of sowing life with our words through intentional confession of the Word of God is simple and easy to understand but it never gets old.

This truth can be put into action by Christians fresh from the cradle, yet remains just as relevant however mature we may grow in our walk with God.

I hope that this book helps you appreciate with fresh gratitude to God the power that resides right under your nose. Literally!

Your brother in Christ,

David Lee Martin

CHOOSE YOUR WORDS
CHANGE YOUR WORLD

THE BIBLE IS A BOOK NOT ONLY TO BE READ BUT TO BE SAID

"...HE WILL HAVE WHATEVER HE SAYS." - JESUS, MARK 11:23

While working as a church planter and pastor I was commissioned by my oversight to write and develop an online Bible school.

As Christians, we believe that the Word of God is truth. Period. No mental gymnastics needed. His book is the only one we can 100% rely upon, and the only judgement we can ever make of God is that He is faithful.

Faithful to His Word.

Sarah, impossibly old to bear the promised child, and against all odds took her stand.

> "...she judged Him [God] faithful who had promised." (Hebrews 11:11 KJV)

God was faithful to Sarah and He will be faithful to you.

Her husband, ageing Abe, was no different.

> "He staggered not at the promise of God through unbelief; but was strong in faith, giving glory to God; And being fully persuaded that, what he had promised, he was able also to perform."
>
> — (ROMANS 4:20–21 KJV)

God's promise became His battle cry.

The Bible is a book full of promises.

The Scriptures are fat with revelation.

So many lights are shone on the human condition that there will never be a day when someone has to scratch for a sermon. For thousands of years, this rich treasure trove has yielded new insights.

The Bible truly is the miracle of all miracles. A supernatural product of God's mind and heart translated without error to the page.

Yet, as beautiful and important as each of the subjects covered in Scripture are, and although I strongly recommend that every believer embark on a thorough subject-by-subject study of the Bible, there are certain doctrines that we simply NEED to know.

Some subjects are woven into every aspect of life and faith.

You'll probably survive without knowing whether the children of Israel used either dolphin or porpoise skins in the making of the Tabernacle (Exodus 25:5, AMPLIFIED). You get by without knowing if Paul was the writer of Hebrews or some other awesome dude. But you'll never even begin to taste the victory Christ has for you if you do not understand, and intentionally apply, the doctrine taught in this short book.

What doctrine are we speaking about?

We are speaking about **speaking**.

What the Bible says about the power of the words that we speak is one of the clearest, most powerful, and applicable spiritual principles you will ever grasp.

Once you get it, and start putting it to work, everything changes.

Why?

Because words, spoken from the heart, are how we change things!

I'll come at this from several different angles, and I'm certain that you will quickly see that this is not some side hustle in the Scriptures. It's a central strand in the Christian life, the lifeblood of the life of faith.

The Bible pulls no punches when it declares:

"Death and life *are* in the power of the tongue: and they that love it shall eat the fruit thereof."

— Proverbs 18:21 KJV

Scripture has so much to teach about how to use your words, and their world-changing potential is quite literally right under your nose.

You can use words in a transformative way to engage and take hold of all that Jesus Christ has taken hold of you for.

Allowing God's Word to become the harness that directs your speech may be *THE* most important thing you ever do.

By the time you finish reading, you will know that the Bible is not a book merely to be *read* - it is a book to be *said!*

When you choose to fill your mouth with the firebrands of heaven radical things take place.

Get ready to dig deep into what the Bible teaches about the power of words. Your words.

You're going to discover that God's Word is designed to be read and spoken aloud, from your heart - filling your mouth with powerful truths that will seed your future with God's purpose for your life, your family, and your ministry.

Faith agrees with God, allows truth to form in the combustion engine of the heart, and then releases that internal power through the lips to propel you forward into God's purposes and completely transform your world.

This, my friend, is the most powerful practice you can ever engage in. It is so simple, but will change your life, and define and direct your destiny.

As Solomon says, you will "eat the fruit of your lips."

"A man's belly shall be satisfied with the fruit of his mouth; *and* with the increase of his lips shall he be filled."

— PROVERBS 18:20, KJV

My mission in the next few pages (and they will be few, I don't think verbosity is a virtue) is to thoroughly convince you that **changing your words will remarkably change your world**.

A SPIRITUAL SWORD

The Scriptures tell us that God's Word is a spiritual sword - a sword that the Holy Spirit wields on our behalf, energising our life with divine power.

"For the Word that God speaks is alive and full of power [making it active, operative, energizing, and effective]; **it is sharper than any two-edged sword**, penetrating to the dividing line of the breath of life (soul) and [the immortal] spirit, and of joints and marrow [of the deepest parts of our nature], exposing and sifting and analyzing and judging the very thoughts and purposes of the heart."

— HEBREWS 4:12 AMPLIFIED

"...and [take] **the sword that the Spirit wields, which is the Word of God.**"

— EPHESIANS 6:17 AMPLIFIED

Clearly, the Word of God is powerful. Most of us would certainly agree with that. But to become the conquering weapon in the spiritual world it is intended to be, something important has to happen.

Using another military term, we could say that is not enough to load the gun. You have to pull the trigger to release the explosive potential that lies within.

That is what it is like with the Word of God.

You load your heart by hearing, reading and meditating on the Word of God, but to pull the trigger you have to speak it out of your mouth!

A sword in its sheath is one thing, but it comes into its true purpose when it is unsheathed and wielded skilfully in the hand of a warrior.

You are the warrior, called and armed with spiritual weapons to pull down the strongholds of the evil one and establish the Kingdom purposes of God.

God's Word is the weapon that you wield.

Learning to use the Word intentionally and aggressively against the schemes of the prince of the power of the air *(Ephesians 2:2)* is paramount for a life of purpose and victory. God has not made the process difficult or hard to understand. You do not need degrees in theology to grasp the facts.

You will have what you say.

It is as simple as that.

Not what you say once or twice.

You will have what you say day after day, aligned with God's Word, and often in the face of contrary evidence and circumstances.

That's why it is a fight. One that you are destined to win!

THE BENEFITS OF
APPLYING THE WORD

If you are like most of humanity, you will only consistently discipline your actions if you have an expectation of a beneficial outcome. The pain of staying the same becomes greater than the pain of change, and discipline will carry you across the line.

The promise of six-pack abs inspires one more sit-up.

The promise of a satisfying career drives a huge investment of time, money, and energy into educating yourself in a narrow discipline. You become remarkable in your area of expertise.

Every endeavour is informed by a vision of what's possible, and the desire to attain the reality of that vision.

The promise and expectation of positive results motivate action, propelling you to actually DO something with the truth that you hear.

Before we wade chest deep in the Word, let's remind ourselves of WHY we want to allow *our words* to be shaped by *His Word*.

"Wherefore lay apart all filthiness and superfluity of naughtiness, and receive with meekness the engrafted word, which is able to save your souls.

But be ye doers of the word, and not hearers only, deceiving your own selves.

For if any be a hearer of the word, and not a doer, he is like unto a man beholding his natural face in a glass:

For he beholdeth himself, and goeth his way, and straightway forgetteth what manner of man he was.

But whoso looketh into the perfect law of liberty, and continueth therein, he being not a forgetful hearer, but a doer of the work, this man shall be blessed in his deed.

If any man among you seem to be religious, and bridleth not his tongue, but deceiveth his own heart, this man's religion is vain."

Unless vigorously put to use the message of this book is impotent, powerless to accomplish its purpose. When you put it into practice, miracles will happen.

We can see from the stern warnings in the book of James that merely reading or agreeing with a form of teaching or training does not transform our experience. It is *acting* upon Truth that commands a blessing.

This means you must put your mouth in gear to appropriate the many benefits promised by the Holy Spirit.

Verse 21 encourages the believer to receive with meekness the engrafted Word. The Amplified translation expands on this idea, picturing the Word of God as a living seed that's planted and tended in the inner man:

"...in a humble (gentle, modest) spirit receive and welcome the Word which implanted and rooted [in your hearts] contains the power to save your souls."

— JAMES 1:21 AMPLIFIED

Interestingly, verse 26 gives clear direction *how* we can do this; *bridling the tongue.*

I am going to explain HOW to do this and place tools in your hand that make it possible.

Before we do, here are just a few of the benefits you can expect as you act on what you learn:

- Renewal of the mind, building into your inner man new truths to live by.
- Moulding your vocabulary, harnessing your tongue to speak only those things God (and you) desire for your life.
- Conforming your thoughts and words to His thoughts and Words.
- Giving expression to the mind of Christ in any and all situations.
- Raising your perspective from earthly to heavenly, from below circumstances to above them.
- Banishing wrong thinking, emotions, and negative self-talk, and replacing them with God's own thoughts (our emotions will always follow our thinking, and our thinking will follow the deposit in our heart, and the words of our mouths).

- You will possess an actionable principle you can apply to combat any adversity you face with confidence.
- You will establish Godly boundaries in your life.
- You will vanquish the devil's plans and purposes because you will never be in agreement with him, and his lies cannot be established.
- You will develop new pictures of yourself, ones that are shaped by God's unchanging love for you.
- You will be equipped with the necessary weapons for the Holy Spirit to bring to your remembrance what is needed to overcome any time your mind, body or spirit comes under attack.
- You will know how to bring every thought into captivity and conformity to Christ, resulting in increased spiritual authority in the spirit realm, and success in relationships and ministry.
- You will release and realise health in your flesh and strength in your bones.
- Every part of your being; spirit, soul and body, will be touched and transformed as your tongue is harnessed to work with the Word.

There are many more wonderful benefits that flow from disciplining ourselves to speak the Word only.

I am sure that you already agree, the investment you need to make putting this into practice is more than worth the effort.

Speaking God's Word is genuinely life-changing. It a spiritual principle that will stand the test of time and every challenge that is thrown at it.

Speaking God's Word is not a fleeting fad of teaching, here today and gone tomorrow. As you will see, it is a Genesis principle established in our very first encounter with the Father and remains a fundamental reality for any child of God who wants to walk and live successfully in the Spirit.

WHOSE WORD DO YOU TRUST?

Whose word do you trust?

This is a powerful question.

I have asked many groups, small and large, how they would answer. Not surprisingly, the most popular are "God", "Jesus" or "the Holy Spirit". All good and very noble answers for sure, but not entirely accurate.

The most honest answer hits home far more painfully than we would often like to admit.

The words that have the greatest influence in your life are not God's - they are your own!

The words that proceed from your own lips are the ones you listen to, the ones you believe, and the ones that you act upon.

How do I know this?

The Scriptures teach that

"...from the abundance of the heart the mouth speaks."

— MATTHEW 12:34; LUKE 6:45

Elsewhere we read that:

"...with the heart that man believes."

— ROMANS 10:10

The unguarded words that overflow from your mouth locate what you really believe in your heart.

It is what you *really* believe in your heart that ultimately shapes your perception of reality, and directs your destiny.

This is at once exciting and exposing.

The exposing thing element is that our words often don't align with what we claim to believe.

The exciting part is that now this hypocrisy is brought to light we can do something about it!

WHO'S WAITING
FOR WHO?

Proverbs 18:21 says that the power of life and death is in the devil...

No it does not!

Neither does it say that the power of life and death is in God!

I dare to propose that many of us have often waited for God to release the power of life into a situation, or to eradicate the whispers of death and destruction. "God, please do this." Or "God, please do that."

All the while the power to do so was entrusted to *us*.

"Death and life are in the power of the tongue,
And those who love it will eat its fruit."

— PROVERBS 18:21 NAS

While we were waiting for God, He was waiting for us!

He was waiting for you to speak so he could act on what you say.

It is impossible for Him to act on words of unbelief and words that don't line up with His design for your life. Often, because we choose to agree with all the wrong things and give voice to them, the hands of the Holy Spirit are tied, and His ability to intervene is limited.

God's Word on your lips is a supernatural substance - a spiritual power that the Holy Ghost is waiting to take hold of and wield on your behalf.

THE GAP BETWEEN
FACT AND TRUTH

B ut how can I speak God's Words when they are
clearly not a reality in my life?

This is also a very pertinent question.

Looking at our circumstances sometimes leaves us in a
dilemma.

There is often a gulf between our circumstances (the facts)
and what God has promised (the reality and the truth).

The question for us is how do we bridge that gap?

I think I have the answer for you, and thankfully it is one
that you can put into motion within minutes.

**The way to bring the facts and circumstances of your
existence closer to the Truth and promises of God is
through your intentional use of words.**

Read that sentence again, slowly and deliberately, and allow the significance of the words to sink in.

Make them personal...

"The way I bring the facts and circumstances of MY existence closer to the Truth and promises of God is through MY intentional use of words."

ENTERING INTO THE
PROMISES OF GOD

L ook at Romans chapter ten.

The Holy Spirit writes;

> "...with the mouth confession is made unto
> salvation."

That tiny word *'unto'* denotes *'entrance into'* and *'moving
towards'*.

For us to 'enter into' and 'move toward' the reality of
God's promises being manifest in our life, we must

activate both faculties of the faith life; The **heart** and the **mouth**.

The heart believes the promises of God, the mouth speaks forth those promises. It does not get simpler than that.

F.F. Bosworth, author of the classic 'Christ the Healer' wrote,

---

"The Word is lifeless until faith is breathed into it on your lips. Then it becomes a supernatural force."

If you want God's Word to become a supernatural force in your life, rather than just a desirable doctrine or distant hope, life must be breathed upon the promises through your own lips.

If you want *God's* Word to take first place in your life, it must first become *your* Word!

His Word must become *your word*.

Moving toward the realisation of Truth in our lives, where Truth becomes an experience, begins in the heart and on the lips.

Jesus and His Word
Are One

Before we begin digging into the high priestly ministry of Jesus, I want to preface with a profound truth that in many ways is a mystery. There are some things we can only comprehend through the Spirit, and this I believe is one of them.

Jesus and His Word are one and the same thing.

I no way do I want to take away from the unique relationship that is necessary for a fulfilling and satisfying Christian walk.

Jesus is a man. He is also God. We can know Him, and walk with Him in sweet fellowship every day of our lives.

Mere words cannot replace this vital reality.

There are many people today, sincere believers, who thoroughly study and adhere to the Bible, but sadly have no real relationship with its author.

As Paul contended, ""Who also hath made us able ministers of the new testament; not of the letter, but of the spirit: for the letter killeth, but the spirit giveth life." (2 Corinthians 3:6 KJV)

This new covenant is not one of mere words, although they are needful, it is one of Spirit and life.

We need both Word and Spirit to be at work in our hearts to see reality.

When you recognize that God's Words and His Person are one it is explosive. Suddenly we are empowered to bring Jesus and His devil-crushing presence onto the scene, and the ability to do so is as close as our breath. We are not waiting for Him to turn up on the scene, he is in our hearts, and in our mouths (Romans 10:8).

Consider for a moment the following Scriptures, and ponder the spiritual implications that they put forth, and how this applies to us today.

I will state them here with minimal commentary as they really do speak for themselves.

The WORD is GOD, and was made flesh.

> **"In the beginning was the Word, and the Word was with God, and the Word was God.** The same was in the beginning with God. All things were made by him; and without him was not any thing made that was made. In him was life; and the life was the light of men... And **the Word was made flesh, and dwelt among us**, (and we beheld his glory, the glory as of the only begotten of the Father,) full of grace and truth.
>
> — JOHN 1:1–4 KJV

THE WORD that God speaks is alive, full of power, and nothing is concealed from HIS sight.

"For **the Word that God speaks is alive and full of power** [making it active, operative, energising, and effective]; it is sharper than any two-edged sword, penetrating to the dividing line of the breath of life (soul) and [the immortal] spirit, and of joints and marrow [of the deepest parts of our nature], exposing and sifting and analyzing and judging the very thoughts and purposes of the heart. **And not a creature exists that is concealed from His sight, but all things are open and exposed, naked and defenseless to the eyes of Him with Whom we have to do.**"

— HEBREWS 4:12–13 AMP

JESUS' name is THE WORD OF GOD.

"...**his name is called The Word of God.**"

— REVELATION 19:13 KJV

The WORD OF GOD is pure, HE is a shield to those who trust in HIM. Declaring His words with precision lifts the shield of faith. This is the strong tower we run into (Proverbs 18:10) because is name (person) and word are one.

"Every WORD OF GOD *is* pure: HE *is* a shield unto them that put their trust in him. Add thou not unto his words, lest he reprove thee, and thou be found a liar."

— PROVERBS 30:5–6 KJV

There are many more references that further confirm this vital truth, but I will allow you to do your own research. Suffice to say, when we deal with God's word in the spirit, we are dealing with God the Son Himself.

"If ye abide in me, and my words abide in you, ye shall ask what ye will, and it shall be done unto you."

— JOHN 15:7 KJV

As far as Jesus was concerned He and His words are inseparable. They are one.

Engaging With Jesus Today

We hear much about the life and ministry of Jesus on earth. But He is no longer walking the dusty shores of Galilee.

We have sermons galore about the cross, and the glorious results of the sacrifice that Jesus made. But, thank God, Jesus is no longer on the cross. For us to follow Him we must take leave of the cross and head on toward the resurrection.

Peering into the tomb we still do not find our Lord. The angel plainly asks, "Why are you looking for the living among the dead? He is not here."

Running to the mount, maybe we will find Him speaking of the Kingdom and His glory?

Even here, our Lord is absent. Maybe we could join the small band of disciples staring up into the clouds, mouths agape in amazement. But again, God soon sends His angels to move us on.

So where do we go to engage with Jesus Christ and His present day ministry?

We must operate from a higher place, one where we are seated together with Him in heavenly places.

But how do we do this?

It should come as no surprise that the answer is through the words that you choose to speak.

How to engage with the risen Jesus and His present-day high priestly ministry is clearly taught in the Scriptures.

Let's take a look and see what the good Book says.

The High Priest Of
Our Confession

We will begin our excavation of rock-solid truth with a few verses to set the stage.

Now the main point of what we have to say is this: **We have such a High Priest**, One Who is seated at the right hand of the majestic [God] in heaven..."

— Hebrews 8:1 AMPLIFIED

Wherefore, holy brethren, partakers of the heavenly calling, **consider the Apostle and High Priest of our profession (confession)**, Christ Jesus;"

— HEBREWS 3:1 KJV

Seeing then that we have a great High Priest who has passed through the heavens, Jesus the Son of God, **let us hold fast our confession.**"

— HEBREWS 4:14 NKJV

Paul says that the sum of all he had previously said to the Hebrews was this one truth - **we have a High Priest in Heaven.** This, he stressed, was the main point his readers needed to grasp.

And it is something we need to grasp too.

Knowing how to effectively engage with Jesus' present-day ministry is essential for our progress in God. Thankfully, these verses also make the mode of His operation very clear - **He is the High Priest of our 'confession'.**

He releases His authority and blessing in proportion to the release of our faith-filled confession.

Jesus' activity in our life is determined by the words we give Him to work with. These two things are intimately connected.

Of course, it should also be noted that negative words, and words that are not in agreement with what God has already spoken over our lives, not only nullify the ability of God to intervene, they play directly into the hands of negative forces. Dark forces seize upon those wrong words and use them aggressively against us, and against God's purposes being worked out in our lives.

This is one more reason to exercise strict discipline in this spiritual arena.

SAY THE SAME
THING AS

D igging a little deeper we can even more accurately understand what is being said in these verses concerning the High Priestly ministry of Jesus on our behalf.

To do that we need to take a look beneath the text at the original Greek, particularly at the word translated 'confession' (or 'profession' in some versions).

The word is *homologia* (Strongs #3671) (*homologia* from *homoú* = together with + *légo* = say)

It literally means **"To say the same thing as"**, Or **"to say together with"**.

And who are we to say the same thing as? God of course!

Not only that. We know where to find what He said. His Words are recorded in the Scriptures.

This, my friend, is where the power of transformation resides.

When we align our words with His we receive the full backing and authority of Jesus, our High Priest.

This is not some hocus-pocus new-age technique. We cannot just pull a fanciful desire out of the air and begin saying over and over again, *"I win the lottery, I win the lottery"*.

The spirit of faith does not work in an arbitrary way. There are clear guidelines and spiritual principles, which, when understood and put into effect, bring God on the scene and give Him permission to act on our behalf and accomplish the impossible.

In the next section, I am going to pull these guidelines apart so we can tear the meat from the bones of them together and see how we can apply them in our lives on a day-to-day basis.

THE POWER OF LIFE
AND DEATH

Death and life are in the power of the tongue, and they who indulge in it shall eat the fruit of it [for death or life]."

— PROVERBS 18:21

I t is a sobering thought to realize that every word that proceeds from your mouth is a seed that will one day grow up, and whose fruit you will eat.

Essentially, this means that **you are eating today what you planted yesterday, and you will taste tomorrow what you plant today**.

The question you need to ask yourself is this, am I planting the kind of life I want I want to experience in my future, or am I planting death and disappointment? The power for both is right now in your own mouth.

Jesus spoke of this again and again. Some of the most quoted verses are found in Mark chapter 11.

"So Jesus answered and said to them, "Have faith in God.

For assuredly, I say to you, **whoever says** to this mountain, "Be removed and be cast into the sea,' and does not doubt in his heart, but believes that **those things he says** will be done, he will have **whatever he says**.

Therefore I say to you, whatever things you ask when you pray, believe that you receive them, and you will have them."

— MARK 11:22-24 NKJV

I want you to notice a few things here.

Number one, we are told to have faith in God. These words can also be rendered, "have the faith *of* God". In fact, this is precisely how God Himself works - He speaks from the rich deposit in His heart, and it springs into being. From the very first verses of Genesis, this is shown to be His clear mode of operation.

Right from the outset we see how

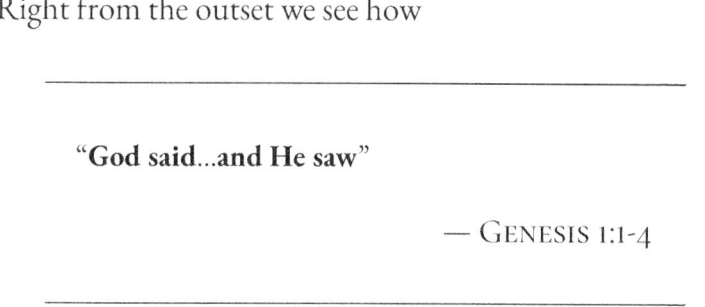

"God said...and He saw"

— GENESIS 1:1-4

We need to first be bold enough to **say something** if we want to **see something**.

The saying comes first - the seeing follows.

God already perceived on the inside what He was about the speak into being, but it was the release of His Words that brought it into existence.

We are encouraged, as those created in God's image and endowed with the supernatural faculty of language, to do the same.

Secondly, take a look at how many times Jesus emphasises the power of words.

"For assuredly, I say to you, whoever **says** to this mountain, "Be removed and be cast into the sea,' and does not doubt in his heart, but believes that those things he **says** will be done, he will have whatever he **says**."

Mark 11:23

Consider especially the final statement, "**he will have whatever he says**".

You will have whatever you say!

This is like God handing you a blank check. Whatever you can believe from His Word and boldly declare can be yours.

Let's get another witness from the Word.

Turn to Joshua chapter 1 verse 8:

> "**This book of the law shall not depart out of thy mouth**; but thou shalt **meditate therein day and night, that thou mayest observe** to **do according to all that is written therein**: for then thou shalt make thy way prosperous, and then thou shalt have good success."
>
> — JOSHUA 1:8 KJV

Let not the Word depart from your mouth (that means keep it in your mouth at all times) that you may observe (see with your own eyes) to do (experience what you are seeing and saying).

If I were a spiritual mathematician I would say that this is a pretty good equation. We say, we see and it equals experience.

Joshua was told to meditate on the words of Scripture. Here again, let me point something out. Meditate does not mean sitting under a tree cross-legged humming your way to heaven.

The literal meaning does include thinking upon, imagining, and pondering, but the emphasis of the word *'haga'* in Hebrew is to utter or mutter. To say. Roll those words over not just in your mind but also in your mouth.

That's why mouth and meditation are coupled together in God's command to his chosen.

And through saying an inner picture will take form giving substance to the things you are meditating upon.

As Paul said,

"...we do not look at the things which are seen, but at the things which are not seen. For the things which are seen are temporary, but the things which are not seen are eternal."

— 2 CORINTHIANS 4:18 NKJV

Our inner man apprehends the things God has promised long before they are manifest.

Say > See > Do (experience)

A simple formula and one that works every time.

Speak To The Mountain, Not About The Mountain

I want to pick on a third and very pertinent point that Jesus makes with regard to His teaching recorded in the book of Mark:

"For assuredly, I say to you, **whoever says to this mountain, "Be removed and be cast into the sea,'** and does not doubt in his heart, but believes that those things he says will be done, he will have whatever he says."

Mark 11:23

Jesus told us to speak *to* the mountain, not *about* the mountain.

A mountain is something that refuses to be ignored. It stands in your way, a stubborn obstacle in your path. At times, it will insist that it is insurmountable, impossible to conquer.

The temptation is to agree with the testimony of that mountainous problem or circumstance and speak about it with everyone we meet. We talk and gossip about how terrible our problem is; how this sickness is killing us, or how the bills are piling up and we do not have the means to pay them.

Don't misunderstand me, I am not saying that it is easy to keep your tongue when circumstances press into your emotions. We need the grace of God intensely in the midst of such battles.

But Jesus taught us not to speak endlessly about our problems. Our vocabulary with regard to these mountains needs to be very to the point; "Be removed!"

Two words.

How many words have you rehearsed about the mountains in your life?

More than two I suspect.

Perpetuate or Annihilate

Our testimony will either agree with the problem or agree with the solution.

You can either **perpetuate** the problem by speaking it over and over again, or you can **annihilate** the problem by speaking the solution as found in the Word of God.

It seems contrary to reason to speak the opposite of what is afflicting us, but God's ways are not the ways of men. Sometimes the foolishness of faith is the solitary path you have to walk if you want to raze that mountain to the floor.

Outer and Inner

And we are not just talking about obstacles outside of ourselves. Sometimes those are actually easier to deal with. For many of us, it is the deep-rooted issues of the soul that keep us bound to old ways and patterns.

Thankfully, the same solution applies to both outward obstacles and inward challenges.

However immovable or deep-rooted they seem, they are no match for the Word of God spoken from the heart.

"And the Lord said, If ye had faith as a grain of mustard seed, ye might **say unto this sycamine tree, Be thou plucked up by the root, and be thou planted in the sea**; and it should obey you."

— LUKE 17:6 KJV

Intentional words of faith spoken from the heart **root out everything contrary to God's perfect will**, replacing them with healing, wholeness, peace and victory.

There is no place too deep or too high and mighty that God's Words on your lips are not powerful enough to overcome and overturn.

Do You Say What You Have or Do You Have What You Say?

J esus did not tell us to *"say what we have"*. He said that we would *"have what we say"*.

These are two very different propositions.

Too often we spend all of our energy and attention saying what we have (or do not have!) rather than spending that same breath on establishing those things that we want based on God's promises.

Scripture tells us that it is through agreement and decree that we establish a thing.

"Thou shalt also decree a thing, and it shall be established unto thee: and the light shall shine upon thy ways."

— JOB 22:28

...**at the mouth** of two witnesses, or at the mouth of three witnesses, shall **the matter be established.**"

— DEUTERONOMY 19:15

Let God's Word be the first witness in any matter, and let your lips be the second establishing witness.

As you put His Word on your lips Heaven and Earth agree, and power is released to affect change in the situation you are addressing.

It is also worth noting that Jesus did not tell us to say what we don't have. An example would be if we are experiencing the symptoms of sickness. Jesus didn't teach his disciples to say, *"I'm not sick, I'm not sick."* That would be a lie. The Bible teaches us to replace natural words with supernatural Truth. We don't say, "I'm not sick", we say "I'm healed by Jesus stripes".

Natural laws are real and we are not denying that. We are however accepting and inviting that a higher law exists, a greater and more powerful reality.

A hunk of metal cannot fly. The force of gravity dictates that. It's a fact.

But there is another law, the law of lift, that when applied according to design defies what previously seemed impossible. The plane soars above the clouds.

Natural law is like gravity. It keeps us earthbound and subject to what the Bible terms "the law of sin and death." But God's Word is our law of lift, taking us high above the dictates of natural living and into the supernatural. The law of the Spirit of life in Christ Jesus gives you wings.

"For **the law of the Spirit of life in Christ Jesus has made me free** from the law of sin and death."

— Romans 8:2 NKJV

His word is the law. Not ours. Positive speaking will take you some way. Even secular psychologists agree on that. But we are not talking about positivity here. We are talking about power. Real power to affect real change. God's word is that power.

Let the importance of these distinctions sink in.

You will have what you say.

We do not say what we have in the natural.

Nor do we lie about what we do not have pretending something isn't so.

Instead, we apply a higher law, addressing the natural circumstances with a more powerful supernatural reality.

In order to experience this, you deliberately choose to stop saying what you have or don't have and instead speak only those things you desire to see come to pass as promised in God's Word.

Maybe right now your life seems like the early words of Genesis, with darkness swirling all around you, and deep problems assailing the void in your soul.

The answer to your dilemma has never changed. Look the darkness straight in the face, and speak the light!

Righteousness Has A Voice

L et's now roll back around to Romans chapter ten. Such amazing words.

We'll joyfully unpack and apply this truth together.

But **the righteousness which is of faith speaketh** on this wise, Say not in thine heart, Who shall ascend into heaven? (that is, to bring Christ down from above:)

Or, Who shall descend into the deep? (that is, to bring up Christ again from the dead.)

But what saith it? The word is nigh thee, even in thy mouth, and in thy heart: that is, the word of faith, which we preach;

That **if thou shalt confess with thy mouth** the Lord Jesus, and shalt believe in thine heart that God hath raised him from the dead, thou shalt be saved.

For **with the heart man believeth** unto righteousness; and **with the mouth confession is made unto** salvation.

For the scripture saith, Whosoever believeth on him shall not be ashamed."

— Romans 10:6-11 KJV

The Holy Spirit not only tells us that righteousness has a voice, but He also tells us how this right standing with God will speak.

A life aligned with God, as received through faith in Jesus Christ, is yours right now. This privileged position and understanding that we have as believers should shape how we speak.

Paul makes it clear that a proper understanding of our position in Christ does NOT say, "Jesus, come down".

How often have we heard, or even prayed this way ourselves? "Come Lord Jesus, Come down in our midst, come into this or that circumstance?"

But the Scriptures here teach us a better way. An unfailing avenue to usher God's presence and power into any situation.

Paul also tells us that righteousness does not say, "Jesus, come up!"

I guess this refers to the kind of sentiment that laments, "If only Jesus were here now, if only He could touch me" and so on. "Touch me, Jesus. Touch me, Jesus."

Jesus has touched you! Even more than that, He has taken up residence inside you. How touched do want to be? How much closer do you honestly think He can be to you? You are already one spirit with Him (1 Corinthians 6:17). That's a close as it gets.

So righteousness (and according to 2 Corinthians 5:21 you are the righteousness of God in Christ Jesus) does not say, "Jesus, come down" or "Jesus, come up".

What does it say?

Righteousness says,

"Jesus is Here!"

"Jesus is right here, right now - in my heart and in my mouth!"

How? Through the spoken Word.

Jesus and the Word of God are one.

As Solomon says in Ecclesiastes 8:4:

"Where the word of a king is, there is power..."

When we speak the Word, we immediately connect with His authority, and His High Priestly ministry, bringing His victory to bear upon any situation or circumstance we speak to.

Words Become Things

"O generation of vipers, how can ye, being evil, speak good things? For **out of the abundance of the heart the mouth speaketh**.

A good man out of the good treasure of the heart **bringeth forth** good things: and an evil man out of the evil treasure **bringeth forth** evil things." (Matthew 12:34 KJV)

Again we see the close relationship the Bible draws between the heart and the lips (the words that we speak).

Whatever your heart is full of, your mouth will spill out.

Your heart is like the soil that receives whatever words are planted in it, for good or for bad. And like any seed that is sown, it grows up and multiplies. It brings forth fruit. The fruit of what is planted in the heart are the words that the mouth eventually speaks. It takes time and cultivation, but is inevitable. What you sow you will reap.

Jesus here describes the process and explains that from the heart the mouth will speak, and that your words will bring things forth!

What is invisible and intangible, becomes visible as it is spoken consistently into existence from the heart.

The system is a lot like the water cycle. Words are deposited in the heart through hearing them spoken, the heart is filled and overflows, and then the mouth speaks from that overflow. The words that are spoken are then heard by the ears and deposited in the heart, and so on.

If we have been untoward or unruly with the words we have chosen to hear and speak maybe this negative cycle needs to be interrupted and a new set of truths set in motion.

Sending The Word To Accomplish

The Holy Spirit alludes to this picture in Isaiah 11:

"For My thoughts are not your thoughts, Nor are your ways My ways," says the LORD.

For as the heavens are higher than the earth, So are My ways higher than your ways, And My thoughts than your thoughts.

For as the rain comes down, and the snow from heaven, And do not return there, But water the earth, And make it bring forth and bud, That it may give seed to the sower And bread to the eater,

So shall My word be that goes forth from My mouth; It shall not return to Me void, But it shall accomplish what I please, And it shall prosper in the thing for which I sent it."

Isaiah 55:8 NKJV

Note that it is the word "that goes forth from My mouth" that accomplishes what is pleasing, and prospers in the thing for which it was sent.

To speak is to send. You send the words you speak. They are sent to accomplish the very thing they say.

What are your words accomplishing for you today?

The determiner is what we choose to put into our hearts and allow to be spoken from our mouths.

Luke 8:11 says that words are seeds. The fruit we eat and enjoy in life will be absolutely determined by the seed that we sow.

God's Words are life and health.

"My son, **attend to my words; incline thine ear unto my sayings.**

Let them not depart from thine eyes; **keep them in the midst of thine heart.**

For they are life unto those that find them, and health to all their flesh.

Keep thy heart with all diligence; for out of it are the issues of life.

Put away from thee a froward mouth, and perverse lips put far from thee."

Proverbs 4:20-24

Notice the cycle:

Attend to God's Word by inclining your ear to hear them. Through your eyes and ears deposit God's Words in your heart, filling your spirit with life and health.

Then, as you keep and fill your heart in this way, it will issue forth life, and wrong speaking will be put away from you.

Your mouth will minister words of life, which in turn will continue the cycle of life-giving, fruit-bearing, supernatural living.

YOU ARE THE PROPHET
OF YOUR OWN LIFE

At times, we can think that the words from someone else's mouth are more powerful than our own. We can hunt for words from the mouth of some great preacher or a prophecy from another renowned prophet. But, believe me, as powerful and life-changing as those words may be, they are nothing in comparison to the words that you hear spoken from your own mouth.

And when you fill your heart and mouth with God's perfect Word, His spiritual life-cycle will go to work in your life to refresh, strengthen, change, transform, and make fruitful every area of your life.

As you do, you set the rudder of your life to carry you to the destination God has prescribed for you.

Read chapter 3 of James and you will see just how important this is.

The entire chapter is packed with revelation, but let's just focus on a few verses.

"For we all often stumble and fall and offend in many things. And **if anyone does not offend in speech [never says the wrong things], he is a fully developed character and a perfect man, able to control his whole body and to curb his entire nature.**

If we set bits in the horses' mouths to make them obey us, we can turn their whole bodies about.

Likewise, look at the ships: though they are so great and are driven by rough winds, they are steered by a very small rudder wherever the impulse of the helmsman determines. **Even so is the tongue is a little member...**"

— JAMES 3:2-5

Your tongue is the rudder of your life.

If you are not heading in the direction you want, you need to change the words that you are speaking.

And as with any ocean voyage, your life will face tremendous challenges and storms at times. It is at these times the winds and the waves will pull and tug at your ship, goading you to weaken your grip and yield to their pressure - in our case say things contrary to the direction and destination set before us in the Word of God.

For this reason, it is essential that you strengthen your spiritual muscles when the seas are open, and the sailing is plain. Don't wait for the storms before you learn to steer your ship and tame your tongue (with God's help and guidance of course).

As you confess God's Word it will shape your speaking, and when the hard times come your rudder will be set, and unyielding to the forces that come against it.

WALKING BY FAITH

I think by now we have established that this principle is found throughout the New Testament.

Paul says we are to "walk by faith, not by sight" (2 Corinthians 5:7).

But how do we do that? What does the Bible teach about walking by faith, and what's the problem with walking by sight?

These are questions I asked the Holy Spirit myself and His answer is plain and simple.

Sometimes people want to spiritualise things so much, make them so mysterious, that ordinary folk like you and I feel that they are out of reach. That is not how the Holy Spirit works.

Anyone close to me knows that I believe in encounters with God, in visions and dreams, and all of the supernatural manifestations of God's presence and gifts as seen in the Bible, and I believe that they are for today, not relegated to obscurity by some dispensational doctrine that says that they passed away.

But all of these things are not how we walk by faith. We do not need a vision or a dream. We don't even need a dramatic encounter or to fast, pray and speak in tongues for several hours a day, to walk by faith. Don't misunderstand, I pray a lot. I speak in tongues constantly. I eagerly expect visitation and encounter, and thirstily drink in God's beautiful presence whenever and wherever I possibly can.

But the Bible teaching about walking by faith boils down to a very easy-to-understand truth.

In fact, walking by faith according to the Bible, is so simple that anyone who chooses to apply it can do so in every situation they face. From the moment you are born again, you can operate as a fair dinkum walking-by-faith-believer.

"We **having the same spirit of faith**, according as it is written, **I believed, and therefore have I spoken**; we also believe, and therefore speak;"

— 2 CORINTHIANS 4:13

The spirit of faith does two things: **believes** and **speaks**.

To walk by faith is to walk by your believing and your speaking.

That's it. It really is that simple.

Hebrews 11:1-3 teaches that faith gives substance to the things that we hope for. It pulls the invisible unrealities of hope and gives substance to them. Our world is framed by His Word, and our faith is released to accomplish His will whenever we release His Word from our mouths.

"Now faith is the substance of things hoped for, the evidence of things not seen. For by it the elders obtained a *good* testimony.

By faith we understand that the worlds were framed by the word of God, so that the things which are seen were not made of things which are visible."

— HEBREWS 11:1-3 NKJV

The word translated 'framed' here is Strongs #2675 *katartizo.*

It carries the idea of *completion, preparation of true purpose, destination or use, bring into its proper condition (whether for the first time, or after a lapse), adjust to be in good order, to fully function - to equip, fully train, to make thoroughly complete, mend (what has been broken or rent) or restore.*

Hebrews 11:1 also contains another powerful key; **"Now"** faith is...

Faith calls those things that are not yet, as if they are already so (Romans 4:17). When faith prays, it believes that it receives NOW those things it prays for (Mark 11:24).

The weak do not look at their weakness, instead, despite what they see, they say that they are strong (Joel 3:10).

When Jesus spoke, He did not do so to merely give us information - His Words were spoken to release the power and potential of Heaven in the earth. Every Word is pregnant with God's power, and we are invited to take hold of those Words, receive them in our hearts, and experience them for ourselves. His Word is a creative force.

The key is to receive them for yourself. All of God's promises are "Yes!" in Christ Jesus, are you going to add your "Amen"?

"For all the promises of God in Him are Yes, and in Him Amen, to the glory of God through us."

— 2 CORINTHIANS 1:20

I believe we bring our agreement, our "Amen", by personalising the promises of God as given through Christ and speaking them out as already ours.

I think you can see easily how powerful this when it is practiced consistently.

Don't Dissect The Bible

I am a big fan of systematic theology - formulating Biblical teaching on different subjects so we can get a proper understanding. The problem is, in seeking to rightly divide the Word of truth, we sometimes dissect things and miss the broader holistic message and testimony originally intended.

For years, my wife and I have taken the New Testament Scriptures relating to what is said about who we are 'in Christ' and made them our confession.

This is a powerful practice.

What struck me recently though, is that the New Testament was not written split into chapter and verse. The letters were written as a complete thought, and in between our favourite verses to quote and claim, that there is a wealth of life that God wants to establish in our inner man.

It led me on a fresh and wonderful journey, revisiting the letters of the New Testament, and personalising them - applying them to my own life and confession.

Taking those words, as spoken by the Holy Ghost, and making them my own.

I want my lips to line up with the encouragement of Hebrews to 'hold fast my confession', and 'say the same thing as' Jesus has already spoken over my life as a redeemed child of God.

HIS WORD MY WORD

Not only does this process of combing God's Word to personalise its message and then actively, intentionally, and consistently confessing that Word, radically change your thinking and the way you perceive the world, but it also plants that Word deep in your heart.

When challenges come, without thinking, the solution will be brought to your remembrance, and a sword of truth will immediately arise from the abundance of your heart to combat all that is contrary to God's will being established in your life.

My heartfelt prayer is that you will take the words on the following pages of this book, and make them your own. Aggressively fill your mouth with these powerful truths taken directly from God's own Word, and watch as they accomplish the miracles they were sent to bring into being when the breath of life is breathed upon them on your lips.

Boldly Declare The Word of God

You have now laid a thorough foundation.

You've heard the Word, now it's time to do it.

In the following three sections, I have taken the Word of God and turned the prison letters of Paul into powerful personal confessions.

As we have seen, bringing God's Word back to Him gives Him permission to act on your behalf to see those words come to pass.

Like the plane on the runway ready for takeoff you are about to apply a higher spiritual law to your life and circumstances.

To engage the throttle you will need to open your mouth and speak.

From here on is, this book is not intended to be read, it is designed to be SAID.

So let's begin...

[Speak aloud and with confidence. These are God's promises given to you in Christ Jesus. They belong to you today.]

"God's Word is true for me today.

I am who the Bible says I am.

I have what the Bible says I have.

His Word is true, and I believe in my heart and confess with my mouth that Jesus is Lord of every aspect of my life.

As I make these declarations directly from the Word of God, I release faith, and they prosper in that for which they were sent..."

There are three volumes that follow and you are welcome to choose whichever ones you want. Each is intended to used in prayer.

The first is the book of Ephesians, followed by Colossians, and then finally the book of Philippians.

The letters of Ephesians, Philippians, Colossians were all written from prison and yet declare some of the most liberating truths on the pages of the Bible.

My prayer is that in practicing this you will immediately experience the power of it, and not only use the volumes I have provided for you here, but also go to the Word for yourself and personalise other books in a similar way.

Thereby His Word will become your Word, with all the rich benefits that follow.

"Let us hold fast the confession of *our* hope without wavering, for He who promised *is* faithful."

— HEBREWS 10:23 NKJV

THE BOOK OF EPHESIANS

The book of Ephesians is one of the richest resources for the saint of God. Paul's letter contains so much insight into our present position and privileges in Christ Jesus.

Declaring these realities boldly from our mouth is life-changing.

Take the words on the following pages, salt them with your own thanksgiving, and rise to take your place in God's affections and authority.

BOLDLY SPEAK THESE WORDS...

I AM A SAINT...

I am a saint, consecrated and set apart by God.

I'm faithful, loyal and steadfast in Christ Jesus.

God's grace, unmerited favour, and spiritual peace, are mine. I live in harmony, unity and undisturbedness.

I am blessed in Christ Jesus with every spiritual blessing in the heavenly realm.

In his love, God chose me, actually picked me out for himself as his own. He chose me in Christ before the foundation of the world that I should be holy, consecrated and set apart for him.

I am blameless in his sight, above reproach, and I stand before him in love. He foreordained, destined and planned in love for me to be adopted and revealed as his own child through Christ. And he did this according to his own will because it pleased him and was his kind intent.

My life commends his glorious grace, favour, and mercy, to others, a grace that is freely bestowed upon me in his beloved Son, Jesus.

I AM REDEEMED…

I have redemption through his blood – complete deliverance, and complete salvation.

All of my sins are forgiven, every offense, shortcoming and trespass is remitted.

I enjoy the riches and generosity of his gracious favour over my life.

His Grace has been lavished upon me in every kind of wisdom and understanding, practical insight and prudence.

God makes known to me the mystery of his will, his plan, and his purposes.

All of this was God's good pleasure, already planned and set forth in Christ for me.

I am God's heritage and portion, and I have obtained an inheritance in him.

He foreordained that I should be chosen and appointed to live fully in his purpose, in complete agreement with the counsel and design of God's own perfect will.

I'm destined to live for the praise of His glory.

I hear the word of truth, accept the good news of my salvation, and believe in and adhere to Jesus with my whole being.

I am sealed by the Spirit...

I am stamped with the seal of the Holy Spirit.

The Spirit is the absolute guarantee of my inheritance. He is the first fruits, the pledge and foretaste of good things to come – the anticipation of my full redemption and my acquiring complete possession of it – to the praise of his glory.

I do not cease to give thanks.

The God of our Lord Jesus Christ, the Father of glory, grants me the spirit of wisdom and revelation, insight into mysteries and secrets, in the deep and intimate knowledge of Him.

The eyes of my heart are flooded with light.

I know and understand the hope to which He is called me, and how rich is glorious inheritance is in the saints.

I know and understand the immeasurable and unlimited and surpassing greatness of his power in and for me because I truly believe.

I am a believer, not a doubter.

His mighty strength is demonstrated and works powerfully in and through me – the same power He exerted in Jesus Christ when he raised him from the dead and seated to Him at His own right hand in the heavenly places.

I am seated in Heaven...

I am seated with Christ, far above all rule and authority, all power and dominion, and every name that is named.

All things have been put under His feet, and I am in him.

He is the head of my life, and his fullness fills me – the full measure of Him, who makes everything complete, filling every part of my life with Himself.

And I have been made alive, who was once a dead in trespasses and sins.

I am no longer dead in trespasses and sins, and I no longer walk in them.

I do not follow the course and fashion of this world and I am not under the sway and tendency of this present age.

I do not follow the prince of the power of the air.

I'm not obedient to or under the control of any demon spirit.

I'm not disobedient, rebellious, careless or unbelieving.

I do not go against the purposes of God.

I do not live or conduct myself in the passions of my flesh.

My behaviour is not governed by a corrupt and sensual nature.

I do not obey the impulses of my flesh, or the thoughts of my mind – the cravings dictated by my senses and dark imaginings.

I am not under God's wrath because He is rich in mercy toward me!

He loves me with a great, wonderful, and intense love.

I AM DEAD TO SIN AND ALIVE TO GOD...

Even when I was dead in sin, slain by my own shortcomings and trespasses, God the Father made me alive together with Christ.

I am alive in fellowship and union with Jesus, the Anointed One.

I have the very life of Christ Himself – the same new life which raised Jesus from the dead and made Him alive. This resurrection life is mine today!

By His undeserved grace, favour, and mercy, I am saved.

I am delivered from judgement.

I am a partaker of Christ's salvation.

I'm raised up together with Him, and I have been made to sit with Him in heavenly realms. I'm seated right now in the Messiah, the anointed one.

God is now, and through the ages to come, demonstrating in me, the immeasurable, limitless, surpassing riches of his free grace – His unmerited favour, kindness, and goodness of heart toward me in Christ Jesus.

By grace, I am saved through faith.

I am delivered from judgement, and I am a partaker of Christ's salvation.

My salvation is not of myself, not of my own doing, not a result of my own striving; it is the gift of God.

I receive the gift of salvation in every part of my life today.

My place of favour and blessing is not by works, not the result of the fulfilment of any law, and what I could not possibly do for myself, He did for me.

I give God all the glory.

I WALK AND LIVE IN GOD'S PERFECT PLAN
FOR MY LIFE...

I am God's handiwork.

I am His workmanship, recreated in Christ Jesus, born
anew so I might do those good works that He has
predestined and planned beforehand for me.

I am taking paths which He has prepared for me ahead of
time.

I walked completely in the paths, and in the works that He
has prepared, living the good life that He has prearranged
and made ready for me to live.

I am no longer separated from God.

I am no longer excluded.

I'm not a stranger to the covenants of God.

I have an eternal hope.

I am not without God in the world. He is my very own Father.

I've been brought near, by, in, and through the blood of Christ.

He Himself is my peace.

He is my bond of unity and harmony.

Every hostile, dividing wall has been broken down.

Through Jesus, I have access by the Holy Spirit to the Father, and I boldly approach God without fear or condemnation.

GOD LIVES IN ME, AND I LIVE IN HIM...

I am truly a citizen of God's kingdom.

I belong to God's own household.

Jesus is my cornerstone, and I stand upon the foundation of the apostles and the prophets.

I am built together with other believers, and we grow together and continue to rise as a holy temple in the Lord – a sanctuary dedicated, consecrated as sacred to the presence of the Lord.

In Him, and in fellowship with others, I am being built up by the Spirit as a living temple for God himself.

God dwells in me.

I am an heir of God, and a joint-heir together with Jesus Christ.

I share in His divine promises.

I'm a minister of the gospel according to the free grace of God bestowed on me by the exercise of His power in all its effectiveness.

I'm a recipient of the unending, boundless, fathomless, incalculable, and exhaustless riches of Christ – a wealth that no human being could ever have searched out!

Through me, the many-sided wisdom of God in all its infinite variety and innumerable aspects is made known to the angelic rulers and authorities in the heavenlies.

I have the boldness, courage, and confidence of free access – an unreserved approach to God with freedom and without fear.

I do not lose heart, faint or become despondent through fear.

God, out of the rich treasury of his glory, strengthens and reinforces me with mighty power in my inner man by the Holy Spirit.

God Himself indwells my innermost being and personality.

Through faith Christ dwells, settles down, and makes his permanent home in my heart.

I am rooted deep in love and founded securely on love.

I have power, and I'm strong to apprehend and grasp with all the saints the experience of that love; the breadth, length, height and depth of it.

I've come to know, practically and through experience for myself, the love of Christ, which far surpasses mere knowledge.

I am filled through my whole being unto all the fullness of God.

I have the richest measure of the divine presence, and I'm a body wholly filled and flooded with God Himself.

God's power is at work in me to do superabundantly, far over and above all that I dare ask or think – infinitely beyond my highest prayers, desires, hopes or dreams.

I walk and lead a life worthy of the divine calling to which I have been called.

I behave in a manner that is a credit to the summons to God's service.

I live with complete lowliness of mind and humility, with meekness, unselfishness, gentleness and mildness – with patience, bearing with others and making allowances because I love others as Christ loves me.

I am eager and strive to guard and keep the harmony and oneness produced by the Holy Spirit in the binding power of peace.

God is my Father, above all, pervading and living in me.

Grace has been given to me, in proportion to the measure of Christ's rich and bounteous gift.

His presence fills all things, the whole universe, from the lowest to the highest.

I AM AN EFFECTIVE MINISTER OF THE GOSPEL...

I am consecrated and equipped to do the work of the ministry, building up the body of Christ, till we all attain oneness in the faith, and in the comprehension of the full and accurate knowledge of the Son of God.

I arrive at really mature manhood – the completeness of personality which is nothing less than the standard height of Christ's own perfection – the measure of the stature of the fullness of Christ, and the completeness found in him.

I'm no longer a child, tossed to and fro between chance winds of doctrine.

Rather, my life lovingly expresses truth in all things.

I speak truly. I deal truly. I live truly.

Enfolded in love, I grow up in Him in every way – in all things I grow into Him, who is the Head – even Christ the Messiah, the Anointed One.

I'm closely joined and knit together with the body of Christ.

I work properly and function, growing to full maturity and building the body of Christ up in love.

I no longer live as the heathen do in perverseness, vanity and emptiness of soul, and in futility of mind.

My heart is not hard or insensitive. My conscience is not calloused.

I am taught by the Anointing.

I strip myself of my former nature. I put off and discard my old unrenewed self.

I'm constantly renewed in the spirit of my mind – having a fresh mental and spiritual attitude.

I put on the new nature, created in God's image, Godlike in true righteousness and holiness.

I reject all falsity, and I express truths with my neighbour.

I never let the sun go down on my wrath, exasperation, fury or indignation.

I do not leave any foothold for the devil, and I give no opportunity to him.

I do not steal, but I make an honest living with my own hands, so that I may be able to give to those in need.

I let no foul or polluting language, evil word or unwholesome or worthless talk, ever come out of my mouth.

My words are only good, and beneficial to the spiritual progress of others, giving grace and God's favour any who hear me.

I do not grieve the Holy Spirit. I do not vex, offend or sadden Him.

By the Holy Spirit, I was sealed, marked, and branded as God's own – secured for the day of redemption, my final deliverance through Christ from evil and the consequences of sin.

I banish all bitterness and indignation from my life.

I banish wrath, rage and bad temper.

I banish resentment, anger, animosity and quarrelling, brawling, clamour and contention from my life.

I banish slander, evil-speaking, abusive or blasphemous language of any kind.

All malice, spite and ill will, or baseness of any kind, is banished from my life.

I am useful, helpful and kind to others – tenderhearted, compassionate, understanding and loving-hearted.

I forgive others readily and freely as Christ forgives me.

I am an imitator of God, I copy Him and follow His example, as a well-beloved child imitates their Father.

I walk in love, esteeming and delighting in others, just as Christ loves me and gave Himself up for me.

I forsake all immorality.

I forsake all sexual vice and impurity.

I forsake all lustful, rich, wasteful living, and all greediness.

I refuse and reject all filthiness from my life, all obscenity and indecency.

I let no foolish, sinful, silly or corrupt talk, nor coarse jesting, come from my lips.

Instead, I voiced my thankfulness to God.

I practice no sexual vice or impurity in thought or life.

I forsake all covetousness and idolatry.

I do not lust after the property of others, and I am not greedy for gain.

I have an inheritance in the kingdom of Christ and God.

I do not associate with the works, or the workers of darkness, rebellion or disobedience.

For I was once darkness, but now I am light in the Lord.

As a child of light, I walk in the light, as one native-born to the light.

The fruit, affect, and product of the light in my life, consists in every form of kindness, goodness, uprightness of heart, and trueness of life.

I'm kind, good, upright and honest.

I learn by experience what is pleasing to the Lord.

My life is a constant proof and example of what is most acceptable to Him.

I take no part in and have no fellowship with, the unfruitful works of darkness.

Instead, I live my life in a way that exposes, reproves and convicts them.

I am vitally awake and alive to God, risen from the dead.

Christ shines upon me and gives me light.

I look carefully how I walk, living purposefully, worthily and accurately – not as unwise and witless, but wisely, sensibly and intelligently.

I redeem the time, making the most of every opportunity because the days are evil.

I'm not vague, thoughtless or foolish.

I understand and firmly grasp what the will of the Lord is.

I do not get drunk with wine, which is debauchery, but I am ever filled with and stimulated with the Holy Spirit.

I speak out in psalms, hymns, and spiritual songs, making melody with all of my heart to the Lord.

At all times and for everything I give thanks in the name of our Lord Jesus Christ to God my Father.

I'm submissive and humble in heart out of reverence for Christ.

WIVES

The following confessions are for WIVES They can also be prophetically adapted and confessed by those who are single and want to prepare for marriage

———

I am submissive and adapt myself to my own husband as a service to the Lord.

My husband is my head as Christ is the head of the church, and the Saviour of His body.

As the church is subject to Christ, so I am subject in everything to my husband.

My husband loves me as Christ loves the church and gave himself for her, so He might sanctify her, having cleansed by the washing of water with the word.

I'm presented to my husband in glorious splendour, without sport or wrinkle or any such thing.

I am holy and without fault.

My husband loves me as his own body, knowing that he who loves his wife loves himself.

My husband nourishes, carefully protects, and cherishes me, as Christ does the church.

I'm joined to my husband, and we are one flesh.

I respect and reverence my husband.

I notice him, regard him, honour him, prefer him, venerate and esteem him, deferring to him, loving and admiring him exceedingly.

HUSBANDS

The following confessions are for HUSBANDS
They can also be prophetically adapted and
confessed by those who are single and want to
prepare for marriage

———

My wife is subject to me, out of reverence for Christ. She is submissive and adapts herself to me as a service to the Lord.

I'm the head of my wife as Christ is the head of the church, Himself the saviour of the body.

As the church is subject to Christ, my wife is subject to me in everything.

I love my wife as Christ loves the church and gave Himself up for her.

I sanctify her, cleansing her by the washing of water with the word.

My wife is glorious, splendid, without spot or wrinkle. She is holy and faultless, and I love her exceedingly.

I love my wife as my own body, knowing that he who loves his wife loves himself. I nourish, carefully protect, and I cherish her as Christ does the church.

I've left my father and mother, and I'm joined to my wife. We are one flesh.

I love my wife as my very own self.

My wife respects and reverences me.

She notices me, regards me, honours me, prefers and venerates and esteems me. She defers to me, praising me, loving me and admiring me exceedingly.

PARENTS

The following confessions are for PARENTS
They can also be prophetically adapted and
confessed by those who are anticipating having
children in the future

My children obey me in the Lord, as his representative, for this is just and right.

My children honour, esteem and value their parents as precious – fulfilling the first commandment with a promise.

It is well with my children, and they live long on the Earth.

Children

*The following confessions are for **CHILDREN** (of any age!)*

———

I obey my parents in the Lord, as his representatives, but this is just and right.

I honour, esteem and value my parents as precious – fulfilling the first commandment with a promise.

Because of this, it is well with me, and I live long on the Earth.

FATHERS

The following confessions are for FATHERS
They can also be prophetically adapted and
confessed by those who anticipate being a father in
the future.

———

I do not irritate or provoke my children to anger.

I do not exasperate them to resentment.

I rear my children in the training, discipline and the counsel and admonition of the Lord.

The confessions now continue for all

I SERVE JESUS CHRIST...

I'm obedient to those who are my superiors, having respect for them and eager concern to please them. In singleness of motive and with all my heart I serve them as a service to Christ Himself.

In all things I do the will of God heartily and with my whole soul, not with eye service, but as a servant of Christ, rendering service readily, with goodwill, as to the Lord and not to men.

I know that whatever good I do, I will receive my reward from the Lord.

I never use threatening, violent or abusive words, knowing that my Master is in heaven and that there is no respect of persons with Him.

I AM STRONG WITH THE STRENGTH OF GOD...

I am strong in the Lord, empowered through my union with him.

I draw my strength from God, a strength that His boundless might provides.

I put on God's whole armour, the armour of heavy-armed soldier that God supplies.

I successfully stand up against all the strategies and deceits of the devil, knowing that I do not wrestle with flesh and blood, or with physical opponents, but against powers, master spirits, world rulers of this present darkness, against the spiritual forces of wickedness in the heavenly supernatural sphere.

I put on God's complete armour.

I resist and stand my ground in the evil day of danger.

Having done all the crisis demands, I stand firmly in my place. I stand, holding my ground.

I tighten the belt of truth around my loins.

I put on the breastplate of integrity, moral rectitude, and right standing with God.

My feet are shod in preparation to face the enemy with firm-footed stability, with the promptness and readiness produced by the good news of the gospel of peace.

I lift up over all the shield of saving faith, upon which I can quench all the flaming missiles of the wicked one.

I take the helmet of salvation. My thoughts are protected.

I take up the sword of the spirit, the sword that the Holy Spirit wields, which is the word of God.

I pray in the Spirit at all times, on every occasion and in every season, with all manner of prayer and entreaty.

To that end, I keep alert and watch with strong purpose and perseverance, interceding in behalf of all the saints, God's consecrated people.

I have freedom of utterance, and I open my mouth to proclaim boldly the mystery of the good news of the gospel.

I am an ambassador of the gospel, declaring it boldly and courageously.

My heart is consoled, cheerful, encouraged, and strengthened.

The peace of God is mine, with love and faith from the Father, and from the Lord Jesus Christ.

Today, I receive God's grace, his undeserved and unmerited favour.

I love my Lord Jesus Christ with an undying and incorruptible love.

Amen.

THE BOOK OF COLOSSIANS

MADE INTO A PERSONAL DECLARATION OF GOD'S WORD

The book of Colossians is a book of putting off the old, and putting on the new.

The truths you are about to declare will uproot all that hinders you in your walk with God and with others, and firmly establish your present and true identity in Christ.

Take the words on the following pages, salt them with your own thanksgiving, and let God's love and grace touch the very depths of your being.

BOLDLY SPEAK THESE WORDS...

I am a saint...

I'm a saint, consecrated to God.

I'm a believer and a faithful follower of Christ.

Grace, spiritual favour, and blessing are mine, and heart peace from God my Father.

I continually give thanks to God the Father of my Lord Jesus Christ.

My faith is securely in Christ Jesus, and I lean my entire human personality on Him in absolute trust and confidence in His power, wisdom, and goodness.

I have and show genuine love for all God saints, because of the hope of experiencing what is laid up and reserved for me in heaven.

I HAVE HOPE AND GROW DAILY IN THE KNOWLEDGE OF GOD...

I have hope in the Gospel, and the truth of the gospel is bearing fruit and growing by its own inherent power in my life.

The good news of Jesus Christ has been bearing good fruit in my life ever since the first day I heard it and came to know the grace of God in truth.

I know the grace and undeserved favour of God in reality, deeply and clearly and thoroughly. I am accurately and intimately acquainted with it.

I fervently love, in and through the power of the Holy Spirit, who is at work in me.

I'm also filled with the full, deep and clear knowledge of God's will in all spiritual wisdom – comprehensive insight into the ways and purposes of God, and in understanding and discernment of spiritual things.

I work, live, and conduct myself in a manner worthy of the Lord, fully pleasing to Him, and desiring to please Him in all things.

I bear fruit in every good work, and I am steadily growing and increasing in and by the knowledge of God.

My knowledge of God grows fuller and deeper every day, with clearer insight, acquaintance with His presence and truth, and recognition of His voice and ways.

I AM DELIVERED FROM THE DOMINION OF
DARKNESS...

I give thanks to the Father, who has qualified and made
me fit to share the generous portion that is the inheritance
of the saints, God's holy people in the light.

The Father has delivered and drawn me to Himself, out of
the control and dominion of darkness and has transferred
me into the kingdom of the Son of his love.

Through the blood of Jesus, I have my redemption, the
forgiveness of all my sins.

All things were created by Him, and for His pleasure they
were created – through Him all things are held together.

He is my Head, the firstborn from among the dead. He
occupies the chief place and stands first and pre-eminent
in my life, family, and ministry.

God purposed that through Christ Jesus I would be
completely reconciled back to Him.

Through the blood of the cross the Father has made peace and brought me into a place of security, assurance, protection and provision.

I have peace with God right now. I'm no longer estranged and alienated from God.

My attitude of mind toward God is not hostile.

Christ the Messiah has reconciled me to God in the body of His flesh through death, to present me holy and faultless and irreproachable in the Father's presence.

I continue to stay with and the truth, well grounded and settled and steadfast, not shifting or moving away from the hope that rests on and is inspired by the glad tidings of the gospel.

In the gospel, I have become a minister in accordance with the divine stewardship which was entrusted to me – to make the Word of God fully known – the mystery of which was hidden but is now revealed to us, his holy saints.

God was pleased to make known to me the riches of the glory of this mystery – Christ in me, the hope of glory!

Jesus Christ is the one I preach and proclaim, urging and admonishing everyone, and instructing everyone in all wisdom.

I share comprehensive insight into the ways in purposes of God, that I may present every person mature, full-grown and fully initiated, complete and perfect in Christ, the anointed one.

I am mature, full-grown, fully initiated, complete and perfect in Christ, the anointed one.

I work, striving with all the superhuman energy that God so mightily provides, enkindles and works within me.

My heart is braced, comforted, cheered, strengthened and encouraged in Christ Jesus.

I FIND MY PURPOSE IN THE BODY OF
CHRIST...

I am knit together with all other believers in love.

I abound with all the wealth and blessings of assured faith,
and conviction of understanding.

I become progressively more intimately acquainted with,
and I know more definitely, accurately, and thoroughly,
the secret of God, which is Christ, the anointed one.

In Him, all the treasures of divine wisdom, comprehensive
insight into the ways and purposes of God, and all the
riches of spiritual knowledge and enlightenment are
stored up and hidden – and I am in Him. All of these
riches are available to me today.

I stand shoulder to shoulder with my brothers and sisters
in Christ, in orderly array, with firmness presenting a solid
front and steadfast faith in Christ.

I lean my entire human personality on Him in absolute trust and confidence in His power, wisdom, and goodness.

As I have received Christ Jesus the Lord, I walk in Him. I regulate my life and conduct myself in union and conformity to Him.

The roots of my being are firmly and deeply planted in him.

I'm fixed and founded in Him.

I'm continually built up in Him.

I'm increasingly more confirmed and established in faith. I abound and overflow in my faith with abundant thanksgiving.

I see to it that no one carries me off or makes me captive with so-called philosophies, intellectualism or vain deceit.

I do not follow human traditions or men's ideas of the material world, rather than the spiritual world.

I fully regard the teachings of Christ the Messiah.

The Holy Spirit Himself is my teacher.

In Christ Jesus, the fullness of the Godhead dwells in bodily form. He gives full expression to the divine nature, and I am in Him giving expression to that nature also.

In Him, I made full and complete.

I have come to fullness of life, and in Christ I too am filled with the Godhead – Father, Son and Holy Spirit – reaching full spiritual stature.

In Him I am circumcised with a circumcision not made with hands.

My entire corrupt, carnal nature, with its passions and lusts, has been stripped from me.

I was buried with Him in my baptism and raised together with Him to new life through my faith in the working of God as displayed when He raised Jesus from the dead.

I am no longer dead in trespasses and sin.

I am no longer subject to the uncircumcision of my flesh, and I am not moved by sensuality or my sinful carnal nature.

I'm brought to life by God Himself, who has freely forgiven all of my transgressions.

God has cancelled, blotted out, and wiped away every law that was hostile to me and stood against me.

Every law, regulation, decree or demand was set aside, and cleared completely out of my way, when He nailed it to the cross.

I AM NO LONGER SUBJECT TO THE DEMONS, THE FLESH OR THE WORLD...

God has disarmed every principality and power that was ranged against me – making a bold display and a public example of them – triumphing over them through the cross!

No demon spirit can triumph over my life. By the authority of Christ, I rebuke every demonic spirit and command them to go from my life, my family, and my ministry.

I know and live in the reality of the new covenant in Christ.

Through Him, I have been made worthy.

Through Him, I am qualified for the prize.

I hold fast to the Head, from whom the entire body, supplied and knit together by means of its joints and ligaments, grows with a growth that is from God.

I have died with Christ to material ways of looking at things.

I have escaped the world's crude and elemental notions, and its worldly teachings.

I no longer belong to the world, and I do not submit to its rules and regulations.

I do not follow human precepts and doctrines – I follow the truth of God's Word.

I do not indulge the flesh. Instead, I honour God with my spirit, soul, and body.

I have been raised with Christ to a new life.

I share His resurrection from the dead.

I aim at and seek after the rich, eternal treasures, which are above, where Christ is seated at the right hand of God.

I set my mind on the realities of Heaven.

I keep my mind set on what is above, the higher things, not the things of the Earth.

I have died, and my new real life is hidden with Christ in God.

When Christ, who is my life, shall appear, I will also appear with Him in the splendour of his glory.

I kill, deaden and deprive of power, the evil desire lurking in my members – I deaden animal desires and all that is earthly – sexual vice, impurity, sensual appetites, unholy desires, and all greed and covetousness.

I banish idolatry from my life and do not worship my self, or any other created thing.

I am a son of obedience, heeding the voice and the Word of God.

I no longer walk in disobedience nor am I addicted to sinful practices.

I put away and rid myself completely of all these things:

Anger

Rage

Bad feelings toward others

Curses and slander

Foulmouthed abuse

Shameful utterances from my lips.

I do not lie.

I have stripped off the old unregenerate self with it's evil practices.

I clothe myself with the new spiritual self and put on the new man.

I'm ever in the process of being renewed and remoulded into fuller and more perfect knowledge upon knowledge, after the image and likeness of Him who created me.

Christ is my all in all.

He is my everything.

I LOVE GOD, AND I LOVE OTHERS,
SINCERELY AND PASSIONATELY...

I clothe myself as one of God's own chosen ones – his hand-picked representative.

I'm purified, holy and well-beloved by God himself.

I put on behaviour marked by tenderhearted pity, a lowly opinion of myself, gentle ways, and patience.

I am tireless, long-suffering, and I have the power to endure what ever comes with good temper.

I am gentle and forbearing with others.

If I have a grievance with another, I readily pardon them, even as the Lord has freely forgiven me.

Above all these things, I put on love.

I enfold myself with the bond of perfectness, which binds everything together completely in ideal harmony.

I let peace, that soul harmony that comes from Christ, rule and act as umpire – deciding and settling with finality all questions that arise in my mind.

I dwell in the peaceful state to which, as a member of Christ's one body, I was called to live.

I'm thankful, appreciative, giving thanks to God always.

I let the word of God, as spoken by Christ, have its home in my heart and mind.

I allow the truth of God's word to dwell in me in all its richness, teaching and admonishing and training others in all insight and intelligence, and wisdom in spiritual things.

I sing continually and psalms, hymns and spiritual songs, making melody in my heart to God.

His amazing Grace is in my heart.

Whatever I do, no matter what it is, in word or deed, I do everything in the name of the Lord Jesus, and complete dependence upon his Person, giving praise to God the Father through him.

WIVES

The following confessions are for WIVES
They can also be prophetically adapted and
confessed by those who anticipate being a wife in the
future.

———

I am subject to my husband, I subordinate and adapt myself to him, as is right and fitting, and my proper duty in the Lord.

My husband loves me. He is affectionate and sympathetic to me. He is never harsh, bitter, or resentful towards me.

My wife is subject to me. She subordinates herself and adapts herself to me, as is right and fitting and her proper duty in the Lord.

HUSBANDS

The following confessions are for HUSBANDS
They can also be prophetically adapted and
confessed by those who anticipate being a husband in
the future.

———

I love my wife. I'm affectionate and sympathetic toward her. I am not harsh, bitter, or resentful toward her.

Parents

The following confessions are for PARENTS They can also be prophetically adapted and confessed by those who anticipate being a parent in the future.

———

My children obey me in everything, for this is pleasing to the Lord.

I do not provoke or irritate or fret my children. I'm not hard on them, and I do not harass them.

I do not discourage my children.

I do not make them feel morose, inferior or frustrated.

I do not break their spirit; I build their spirit.

CHILDREN

*The following confessions are for **CHILDREN** (of any age!)*

––––––

I obey my parents in everything, for this is pleasing to the Lord.

The confessions now continue for all

I SERVE JESUS CHRIST...

I obey in everything those who are my earthly masters, not as a man pleaser and only when I'm being watched, but in simplicity of purpose and with all my heart. I do this because of my reverence for the Lord and as a sincere expression of my devotion to Him.

Whatever my task, I work at it heartily, as something done for the Lord and not for men.

I know with all certainty, that it is from the Lord, and not from men, that I will receive the inheritance that is my real reward.

Whatever good thing I do for another, I receive myself from Him.

I know that the One whom I actually serve is the Lord Jesus Christ, the Messiah.

I know that I will reap what I sow, so live in a manner that bears good fruit.

I deal with people justly, and fairly, knowing that I have a Master in heaven.

I AM EFFECTIVE IN PRAYER AND MINISTRY...

I am earnest and unwearied and steadfast in my prayer life – I am both alert and intent in my prayers - with abundant thanksgiving.

I pray that God will open a wide and effective door for the Word of God to be proclaimed.

I pray that the gospel will be proclaimed fully and that the mystery of the gospel will be made clear.

I behave myself wisely, living prudently and with discretion in my relations with non-Christians.

I make the most of the time, seizing and buying up every opportunity.

At all times, my speech is gracious, pleasant and winsome, seasoned with salt.

I'm never at a loss to know how I ought to answer anyone who puts a question to me.

I comfort, cheer, and encourage others.

I heartily welcome, love, and support, the servants of God.

I am a person of ripe character and clear conviction. I stand firm and mature in spiritual growth, convinced and fully assured in all the will of God.

I discharge carefully the duties of my ministry and fulfil the stewardship that I've received in the Lord.

God's grace, His unmerited favour and blessing, is with me.

Amen

THE BOOK OF
PHILIPPIANS

The book of Philippians is so vibrant with the overflowing heart of the gospel. As you proclaim its truths over your own life, you will be filled to overflowing with God's supernatural compassion for the world, and His indescribable love for you as one of His chosen vessels.

Take the words on the following pages, salt them with your own thanksgiving, and let the joy of God fill and overflow in your life and ministry.

BOLDLY SPEAK THESE WORDS...

I am a saint...

I am a Saint, and one of God's consecrated people.

I am in Christ Jesus.

I enjoy grace, favour and heart peace from God my Father and the Lord Jesus Christ.

Today and always, I make all my petitions with joy.

I sympathetically cooperate and contribute to the work of the gospel, partnering with God's servants.

I do all I can to advance the gospel of Jesus Christ.

GOD WILL COMPLETE THE GOOD WORK THAT HE HAS BEGUN IN ME...

I'm convinced and sure of this very thing, that He who began a good work in me will continue it until the day of Jesus Christ – right up to the time of his return.

God is developing that good work, and perfecting and bringing it to full completion.

I'm a partaker and a sharer of God's grace, his unmerited favour and spiritual blessing.

My love abounds more and more, extending to its fullest development, in knowledge and all keen insight.

My love displays itself in greater depth of acquaintance and more comprehensive discernment of the ways of God.

I have learned what is vital and I approve and prize what is excellent and of real value.

I recognise the highest and the best, distinguishing the moral differences.

I am untainted, pure, unerring and blameless.

My heart is sincere, certain and unsullied.

I approach the day of Christ, not stumbling no causing others to stumble.

I abound in and I am filled with the fruits of righteousness – the results of right standing with God and right doing.

All of this comes through Jesus Christ, the Anointed One, to the honour and praise of God – that His glory may be both manifested and recognised.

I AM AN EFFECTIVE MINISTER OF THE GOSPEL...

I am bold to speak and publish the Word of God fearlessly, acting with freedom and indifference to the consequences.

I preach Christ out of a loyal spirit and goodwill, motivated by love.

I do not have a political or partisan spirit.

I am sincere in all my dealings.

My motives are pure.

I proclaim Christ in all honesty for the furtherance of the truth.

Through my prayers, there is a bountiful supply of the Spirit of Jesus Christ, which avails toward the saving work of the gospel.

I eagerly desire with persistent expectation and hope that I shall not disgrace myself, nor be put to shame in anything.

With utmost freedom of speech and unfailing courage, Christ is magnified and gets glory and praise in this body of mine.

Jesus is boldly exalted in my person.

For me to live is Christ and to die is gain.

As long as I have life and breath, my service to God will be fruitful.

I promote the spiritual progress of others, and their joy in believing.

I conduct myself in a manner that is worthy of the good news of the gospel of Christ.

I stand firm and united in spirit and purpose, striving side-by-side with my Christian brothers and sisters and contending with a single mind for the faith of the gospel.

I'm not frightened or intimidated by my opponents and adversaries, even for a moment.

I am constant and fearless, unmoved by circumstance, fully trusting in God's faithfulness.

My salvation and deliverance are from God.

I have been granted the privilege for Christ sake, not only to believe in and adhere to Him, relying on and trusting in Him, but also to suffer in his behalf.

I LOVE OTHERS AS GOD LOVES ME...

I dwell together with my brothers and sisters in Christ.

I'm strengthened, consoled and encouraged in my relationship with God and with others.

I am moved and motivated by love.

I participate and share in the Holy Spirit.

I have deep affection and compassionate sympathy for others.

I live in harmony with my brethren.

I'm of one mind with them, one in purpose, having the same love, being in full accord and of one harmonious mind and intention.

I do nothing from factional motives.

I'm not contentious.

I banish strife and selfishness from my life.

I do nothing for unworthy ends, prompted by conceit or empty arrogance.

Instead, in the true spirit of humility and lowliness of mind, I regard others as better and superior to myself.

I think more highly of others than I think of myself.

I esteem and look upon and I'm concerned not merely for my own interests, but also those of others.

I let the same attitude and purpose and humble mind be in me that was in Christ Jesus.

He is my example in humility.

Who, although being essentially one with God, did not think this equality with God thing to be eagerly grasped and retained.

I assume the guise of the servant, humbling myself until I have carried out my obedience to God in full.

As I humble myself God will lift me up, and exalt me together with Christ.

I worship Jesus and bow my knee to him.

I frankly and openly confess and acknowledge that Jesus Christ is Lord, to the glory of God the Father.

GOD IS WORKING IN ME...

I work out, cultivate and carry out to the goal, to full completion, my own salvation with reverence and awe, trembling at God's word.

I live with serious caution, tenderness of conscience, watchful against temptation, timidly shrinking from whatever might offend God and discredit the name of Christ.

I do nothing in my strength, for it is God who is all the while effectually at work in me, energising and creating in me the power and desire both to will and to work for his good pleasure and satisfaction and delight.

I do all things without grumbling, faultfinding and complaining.

I do not question or doubt God's goodness, but do the will of God wholeheartedly.

I show myself to be blameless, guileless, innocent and uncontaminated.

I'm a child of God without blemish.

I'm faultless and unrebukable in the midst of a crooked and perverse generation – among whom I am seen as a bright light – a beacon shining out clearly in this dark world.

I hold out and offer to all men the Word of life.

I rejoice and glory that in the day of Christ I will celebrate that I did not run my race in vain or spend my labour to no purpose.

I am genuinely interested in the welfare of my brethren and devoted to their interests. I do not seek to advance my own interests, but those of Jesus Christ the Messiah.

As a son in the gospel, I serve zealously to advance the good news.

I'M CONFIDENT, FULLY TRUSTING THE LORD...

I welcome joyfully, honour and highly appreciate the servants and fellow ministers of the gospel.

I delight myself in the Lord, and continue to rejoice that I am in Him.

I worship God in Spirit, and by the Spirit of God I glory in Jesus Christ.

I put no confidence or dependence on what I am in the flesh, on outward privileges, physical advantages or external appearances.

Whatever former things I had that might have been gains to me, I've come to consider all as one combined loss for Christ sake.

Yes, I consider everything is loss compared to the priceless privilege – the overwhelming preciousness, surpassing worth, and supreme advantage - of knowing Jesus Christ my Lord, and becoming more deeply and intimately acquainted with him.

I perceive and recognise and understand God more fully and clearly every day.

For Jesus sake I've lost everything and consider it all as mere rubbish, so that I may win Christ, the Anointed One.

I am found and known as in Him, not having any self-achieved righteousness that can be called my own, but possessing the genuine righteousness that comes through faith in Christ, the Anointed One.

I truly have right standing with God, a righteousness that comes from God by saving faith.

I KNOW GOD DEEPLY AND INTIMATELY...

My determined purpose is that I may know Him, that I may progressively become more deeply and intimately acquainted with Him, perceiving and recognising and understanding the wonders of his Person more strongly and more clearly; that I may know the power outflowing from his resurrection, and that I may also share his sufferings and be continually transformed into his likeness.

I have not yet attained this ideal, or have already been made perfect, but I press on to lay hold, grasp and make my own, that for which Christ Jesus has laid hold of me and made me his own.

My one aspiration is to forget that which is behind, and strain forward to what lies ahead – I pressed toward the goal to win the supreme and heavenly prize to which God in Christ Jesus is calling me upward.

I hold true to what I have already attained and walk and order my life by that.

I'm not ruled by my appetites or by sensuality.

I'm a citizen of Heaven and from there I earnestly and patiently await the coming of the Lord Jesus Christ as Saviour.

Through his divine power, He will transform and fashion anew my body, conforming it to be like his glorious body.

I stand firm in the Lord.

I rejoice in the Lord always.

I delight and gladden myself in Him. Again, I say rejoice!

All men know, perceive and recognise my unselfishness, my considerateness, and my forbearing spirit.

The Lord is near – He is coming soon!

GOD IS IN CONTROL OF MY LIFE, AND I TRUST HIM COMPLETELY...

I do not fret or have anxiety about anything, but in everything and every circumstance and every situation, by prayer and petition, I make definite requests with thanksgiving, continuing to make my wants known to God.

I'm anxious for nothing, but in all things by prayer and supplication, I make my requests known to God.

God is my peace.

I live in a tranquil state of soul assured of its salvation through Christ.

I fear nothing from God, and I am content with my earthly lot.

The peace of God which transcends all understanding, garrisons and mounts guard over my heart and mind in Christ Jesus.

Whatever is true, whatever is worthy of reverence and is honourable and seemly; whatever is just, whatever is pure, whatever is lovely and lovable, whatever is kind and winsome and gracious – if there be any virtue and excellence, if there is anything worthy of praise - I think on and weigh and take account of these things, and I fix my mind upon them.

I practice what I have learned, received and heard – being a doer of the word and not a hearer only.

I model my way of life on the truth of the gospel, and on the perfect living Word of God.

The God of peace is with me.

I'm untroubled and I enjoy undisturbed well-being.

I have learned how to be content in whatever state I am.

I am satisfied to the point where I am not disturbed or disquieted by anything.

I know how to abased and live humbly in straitened circumstances, and I also know how to enjoy plenty, and live in abundance.

I've learned in any and all circumstances the secret of facing every situation. Whether well fed or hungry, having enough to spare or going without, I am content and confident in God.

I AM AND HAVE MORE THAN ENOUGH TO
FULFIL GOD'S WILL IN MY LIFE...

I have strength for all things through Christ who strengthens and empowers me.

I'm ready for anything, and equal to anything, through Him who infuses inner strength into me.

I'm self-sufficient with Christ's sufficiency.

I generously give to the gospel, partnering with God's servants, and a fruitful harvest of blessing accumulates to my account.

I have everything I need and I am amply supplied.

My God liberally supplies and fills to the full my every need according to His riches in glory by Christ Jesus.

I give glory to God my Father.

God's grace, spiritual favour and the blessing of the Lord Jesus Christ, the Anointed One, is with my spirit.

Amen.

About the Author

David Lee Martin is a passionate and very imperfect Christian. Although he is an ordained pastor, and the author of the Spirit Life Online Bible School, he chooses to not put too much confidence in those things to shape his identity.

At the end of the day, he is very much like you, a man who has discovered that there really is a gracious God who has called us to know Him in a real and tangible way.

His life vocation is to discover more of the grace that he has tasted, and to share it with as many others as he can.

David is happily married to Larna, and they have four awesome kids.

Here are some other books by David that you may find helpful

All can be found on Amazon

Turn the page to browse...

Wanted – Ferocious Men of Prayer is an uncompromising call for Godly men to rise up in God's purposes and humble their hearts before the Almighty God.

The devil fears nothing more than a man given to prayer.

As the famous preacher and revivalist, Robert Murray McCheyne said, *"A holy man is a fearful weapon in the hands of a holy God."*

Will He find such a man in you?

Read Now on Amazon

DISCOVERING & DEVELOPING A
PASSION FOR GOD

"YOU SHALL LOVE THE LORD YOUR GOD WITH ALL
YOUR HEART, WITH ALL YOUR SOUL, AND WITH
ALL YOUR STRENGTH." DEUTERONOMY 6:5

DAVID LEE MARTIN

As a believer, you have not been called to live a lukewarm Christian life. You were never intended to be an armchair Christian. You've been powerfully anointed to live a life of passion and purpose!

God is seeking those who will call upon His name, and stir themselves to take hold of Him.

Is that you? Are you one of the rare firebrands He is looking for? Let this firebrand book pour fuel on your fire of devotion.

Read Now On Amazon

DISCOVERING & DEVELOPING THE SECRET DEPTHS OF

THE LORD'S PRAYER

"AFTER THIS MANNER THEREFORE PRAY YE:
OUR FATHER WHICH ART IN HEAVEN,
HALLOWED BE THY NAME..." MATTHEW 6:9

DAVID LEE MARTIN

A powerful prayer life does not happen by accident. God has provided pathways to His presence that guarantee growth and intimacy in prayer. The question is, are you taking advantage of them?

David's deep-rooted teaching from the Scriptures will guide you to a Spirit-filled understanding of Jesus' key training in prayer, and open up pathways to intimacy and faith that will radically transform and enrich your times together with God.

Read Now on Amazon

LOVE YOURSELF
LIKE JESUS LOVES YOU
RADICALLY & WITH ALL YOUR HEART

"LOVE THE LORD YOUR GOD WITH ALL YOUR HEART,
AND LOVE YOUR NEIGHBOR AS YOURSELF."
MATTHEW 22:37-39

DAVID LEE MARTIN

You are LOVED!

Love is the heartbeat of our Father. Passion permeates every word He has ever spoken and every deed He has ever done. He created you. You are one-of-a-kind. A child of God. And you are loved.

But the transformative and healing power of God's love for you is only effective when you add the missing ingredient.

What is that ingredient? Find out in *Love Yourself Like Jesus Loves You*.

Read Now On Amazon

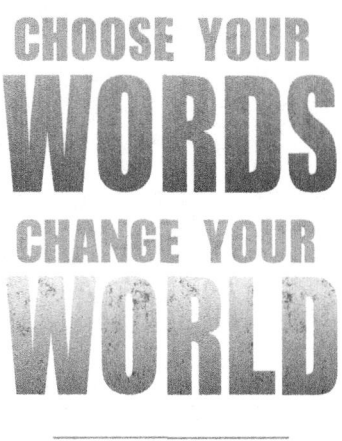

CHOOSE YOUR WORDS CHANGE YOUR WORLD

THE ANSWER YOU'VE BEEN LOOKING
FOR IS RIGHT UNDER YOUR NOSE!

DAVID LEE MARTIN

The Scriptures make plain how we are to **engage with God and release His transforming power consistently in our everyday lives**.

In this practical Spirit-filled book pastor and Bible teacher, David Lee Martin unpacks the amazing truth concerning the power of the words that you speak and **shows clearly how you can apply this truth to change your world and the world of those around you**.

Includes in-depth teaching plus three volumes of Bible-based confessions direct from Scripture.

Read Now on Amazon

SWITCH OFF DISTRACTION AND HEAR THE STILL SMALL VOICE OF GOD

DAVID LEE MARTIN

Amidst the noise and scrolling, a still small voice is speaking. God is here waiting to be known, but His voice and the peace He offers are too often drowned out in the busyness of modern life.

Constant distraction. In this digital age of incessant interruptions, a relentless war is being waged to possess your splintered attention. Digital addictions clamor for another slice of your precious life.

UNPLUG is a call to cut off the digital cacophony and reclaim your peace.

Read Now On Amazon

FEARLESS Prayer Journal For Men of God includes over 200 inspirational Scripture verses and quotes from great men and women through the centuries to fuel your own fervent prayer life.

You will also enjoy boldly illustrated motivation straight from the Bible, prayer prompts, ample space for your own journaling, and devil-chasing teaching.

Start recording and celebrating your growing relationship with God today.

Get Your FEARLESS Journal On Amazon

Designed especially for women of God this is a personal prayer journal for daughters of the King! A precious place to record your encounters with your Father in Heaven, and equip yourself for victorious living as a much-loved child of God.

Includes: Over 200 inspirational Scripture verses and quotes from great men and women through the centuries, beautifully illustrated motivation straight from the Bible, prayer prompts, abundant space for your own journaling, and plenty of hidden surprises!

Buy this beautifully illustrated and faith-filled journal and start recording and celebrating your growing intimacy with God today.

Get Your FERVENT Journal On Amazon

The Spirit Life Bible School

Please also feel free to sign up for my free Bible school. A complete and comprehensive online school to deepen your knowledge of the Word and your walk with God.

SpiritLife
Bible School

A Free Spirit Filled Online Bible School

Teaching Ordinary People to Live & Walk Every Day With an Extraordinary God If you are hungry to know God's Word, and apply it in your life, then the Spirit Life online Bible School provides everything you need to progress your dream.

Sign up today at JesusChrist.co.uk

ACKNOWLEDGMENTS

Root texts using in preparing these personal declarations include:

Amplified® Bible Copyright © 1954, 1958, 1962, 1964, 1965, 1987 by The Lockman Foundation Used by permission. (www.Lockman.org)

New Living Translation Copyright ©1996, 2004, 2007, 2013 by Tyndale House Foundation. Used by permission of Tyndale House Publishers, Inc., Carol Stream, Illinois 60188. All rights reserved.

New King James Version. Copyright © 1982 by Thomas Nelson, Inc. Used by permission. All rights reserved.

New American Standard Bible® Copyright © 1960, 1962, 1963, 1968, 1971, 1972, 1973, 1975, 1977, 1995 by The Lockman Foundation Used by permission." (www.Lockman.org)

Authorised King James Version, Public Domain

Printed by Amazon Italia Logistica S.r.l.
Torrazza Piemonte (TO), Italy

51189003R00112